Soda Bread Cookbook

Discover the Art of Baking Irish Soda Bread and Beyond

While every precaution has been taken in the preparation of this book, the publisher assumes no responsibility for errors or omissions, or for damages resulting from the use of the information contained herein.

SODA BREAD COOKBOOK

First edition. November 11, 2023.

ISBN: 979-8223518495

Written by Sammy Andrews.

Sammy Andrews

Sourdough Soda Bread

- Combining Two Traditions
- Sourdough Starter Guide

Stuffed Soda Breads

- Cheesy Stuffed Bread
- Savory Filling Ideas

Flavored Soda Bread Spreads

- Homemade Butter
- Jam and Jelly Complements

International Soda Bread Recipes

- American Buttermilk Biscuits
- Australian Damper

Soda Bread in a Pinch

- Emergency Soda Bread
- Quick and Easy Recipes

Soda Bread for Special Occasions

- Holiday Variations
- Soda Bread Stuffing

Baking with Soda Bread Crumbs

- Breadcrumbs and Coatings
- Topping Ideas

Chapter 1: Introduction to Soda Bread

A Brief History of Soda Bread

Soda bread is a classic Irish staple, known for its simplicity, versatility, and distinctive flavor. Before we delve into the delightful world of soda bread recipes and techniques, it's important to understand the history and origins of this beloved bread.

The Origins: Soda bread has deep roots in Ireland, dating back to the early 19th century. It was born out of necessity when baking soda, or bicarbonate of soda, became a readily available leavening agent. Traditional Irish bread, such as the iconic brown soda bread, was initially made with just three basic ingredients: flour, baking soda, and buttermilk.

Why Soda Bread?: The use of baking soda as a leavening agent was particularly suitable for Irish bakers due to Ireland's climate and available resources. Yeast could be unreliable in the damp, cool conditions of Ireland, so soda bread offered a dependable alternative. Additionally, it was a cost-effective way to create a hearty, filling bread.

A Bread for All Occasions: Soda bread quickly gained popularity for its quick preparation and delicious results. It became a staple in Irish households, gracing the tables at breakfast, lunch, and dinner. Soda bread was the perfect accompaniment to a bowl of hearty stew or a simple spread of butter and jam.

Ingredients and Their Roles

To create the perfect loaf of soda bread, it's essential to understand the ingredients you'll be working with and how they contribute to the final product. Here's a breakdown of the key components:

1. Flour: The primary ingredient in soda bread, flour provides structure and texture. In traditional recipes, a mixture of white and

whole wheat flours is often used, but you'll also find variations with rye, oat, and other flours.

2. Baking Soda: Baking soda, also known as bicarbonate of soda, is the leavening agent that makes soda bread rise. When combined with an acidic ingredient, such as buttermilk, it produces carbon dioxide gas, causing the dough to expand and become airy.

3. Buttermilk: Buttermilk serves two crucial roles in soda bread. First, it reacts with baking soda to create the leavening effect. Second, its acidity contributes to the bread's distinct flavor and tender crumb.

4. Salt: A small amount of salt enhances the bread's overall flavor, balancing the sweetness of the buttermilk and adding depth to the taste.

5. Optional Add-Ins: While traditional soda bread is delightfully plain, you can personalize your loaves with optional add-ins like raisins, seeds, nuts, or herbs. These additions bring new flavors and textures to your bread.

Equipment You'll Need

Before you embark on your soda bread baking journey, it's essential to have the right tools at your disposal. Fortunately, you won't need any fancy equipment; the basics will suffice:

1. Mixing Bowl: Choose a large mixing bowl to comfortably combine your ingredients.

2. Measuring Cups and Spoons: Precise measurements are crucial for soda bread, so have a set of measuring cups and spoons on hand.

3. Whisk or Wooden Spoon: You'll need a utensil to mix your dry and wet ingredients thoroughly. A whisk or a wooden spoon works well.

4. Baking Sheet: Most soda bread recipes call for baking on a standard baking sheet. If you're feeling adventurous, you can use a cast-iron skillet for a rustic touch.

5. Knife or Scoring Tool: To create decorative scores on your soda bread before baking, have a sharp knife or a designated scoring tool ready.

6. Cooling Rack: After your bread is baked to perfection, allow it to cool on a wire rack to prevent condensation and maintain its texture.

With these basics in your kitchen, you're well-prepared to begin your soda bread baking adventure. In the upcoming chapters, we'll explore various types of soda bread, from classic white loaves to creative sweet and savory variations. Get ready to enjoy the delightful world of soda bread!

Chapter 2: Classic White Soda Bread

Traditional Irish Recipe

Classic white soda bread is the heart and soul of Irish baking. This humble yet satisfying bread has been a staple on Irish tables for generations. Its simplicity, quick preparation, and delicious taste make it a beloved favorite. In this chapter, we'll explore the traditional Irish recipe for white soda bread, sharing the secrets to achieving that perfect golden-brown crust and tender crumb.

Ingredients
You'll Need:

- 3 cups all-purpose flour
- 1 teaspoon baking soda
- 1 teaspoon salt
- 1 1/2 cups buttermilk (approximately)

Instructions

1. Preheat Your Oven

Preheat your oven to 425°F (220°C). Dust a baking sheet with a bit of flour to prevent sticking.

2. Combine Dry Ingredients

In a large mixing bowl, sift together the all-purpose flour, baking soda, and salt. Sifting helps distribute the baking soda evenly, ensuring uniform leavening.

3. Make a Well

Create a well in the center of the dry ingredients. This well will be the spot where you pour the buttermilk.

4. Add Buttermilk

Slowly pour most of the buttermilk into the well, reserving a small amount. Begin mixing the flour into the buttermilk using a wooden spoon or your hand. Be gentle; you want to combine the ingredients without overworking the dough.

5. Form a Dough

As you mix, the dough will come together. If it's too dry, add a bit more buttermilk until you have a soft, slightly sticky dough. Remember, the exact amount of buttermilk can vary based on factors like humidity and flour type.

6. Shape the Dough

Turn the dough out onto a lightly floured surface. Knead it briefly (about 1-2 minutes) until it forms a round, flat loaf. Avoid excessive kneading; soda bread dough should be handled gently.

7. Score the Loaf

Use a sharp knife to score a deep 'X' on the top of the loaf. This tradition is not just for aesthetics; it helps the bread cook evenly.

8. Bake

Place the scored loaf onto the prepared baking sheet. Bake in the preheated oven for 15 minutes. Then, reduce the oven temperature to 400°F (200°C) and continue baking for an additional 20-30 minutes, or until the bread is golden brown and sounds hollow when tapped on the bottom.

9. Cool and Enjoy

Remove the soda bread from the oven and allow it to cool on a wire rack. Once cooled, slice and serve. Classic white soda bread is best enjoyed fresh, with a generous spread of butter.

Variations on White Soda Bread

Classic white soda bread is a canvas for endless variations. While the traditional recipe is a cherished favorite, you can add your own creative twists. Here are a few ideas:

1. Buttermilk and Herbs: Add a handful of chopped fresh herbs, like rosemary or thyme, to the dough for a fragrant and flavorful bread.

2. Cheesy White Soda Bread: Mix in shredded cheddar or Parmesan cheese for a savory, cheesy twist.

3. Sunflower and Flax Seeds: Boost the nutritional content by incorporating sunflower seeds, flax seeds, or a mix of seeds into the dough.

4. Spices and Dried Fruits: Experiment with a sweet version by adding a pinch of cinnamon and some raisins or currants.

White soda bread is versatile and forgiving, making it the perfect recipe for bakers of all levels. Its simple ingredients and straightforward preparation make it a delightful bread to master. Whether you stick to the classic recipe or venture into creative variations, you're sure to savor the taste of this timeless Irish treasure.

Chapter 3: Whole Wheat Soda Bread

Nutritional Benefits

Whole wheat soda bread is a wholesome and nutritious twist on the classic Irish soda bread. By incorporating whole wheat flour, you not only add a rustic flavor but also boost the bread's nutritional value. In this chapter, we'll explore the world of whole wheat soda bread, discussing its nutritional benefits and providing a delicious recipe for you to enjoy.

Nutritional Benefits of Whole Wheat Soda Bread

Whole wheat soda bread offers several nutritional advantages over its white flour counterpart:

1. Dietary Fiber: Whole wheat flour is rich in dietary fiber, which promotes digestive health, helps maintain a feeling of fullness, and regulates blood sugar levels.

2. Vitamins and Minerals: Whole wheat flour contains essential vitamins and minerals, including B vitamins, iron, magnesium, and zinc, which contribute to overall well-being.

3. Antioxidants: The bran and germ in whole wheat contain antioxidants that help protect cells from damage caused by free radicals.

4. Lower Glycemic Index: Whole wheat bread generally has a lower glycemic index compared to white bread, making it a better choice for those managing their blood sugar levels.

5. Satiety: The fiber and complex carbohydrates in whole wheat bread can help keep you feeling satisfied for longer, aiding in weight management.

Whole Wheat Varieties

Before we dive into the recipe, it's worth exploring the different types of whole wheat flour available:

1. Whole Wheat Flour: This is the most common type of whole wheat flour, milled from the entire wheat kernel.

2. Whole Wheat Pastry Flour: Finer and lighter in texture, this flour is well-suited for baked goods like muffins, cookies, and tender whole wheat bread.

3. White Whole Wheat Flour: While not truly "white," this flour is made from a lighter wheat variety, resulting in a milder flavor and lighter color.

4. Sprouted Whole Wheat Flour: Made from wheat kernels that have been allowed to sprout before milling, this flour is believed to be easier to digest and may have increased nutritional benefits.

Whole Wheat Soda Bread Recipe
Ingredients:

- 2 cups whole wheat flour
- 1 cup all-purpose flour
- 1 teaspoon baking soda
- 1 teaspoon salt
- 1 1/2 cups buttermilk (approximately)

Instructions:
1. Preheat Your Oven
Preheat your oven to 425°F (220°C). Dust a baking sheet with a bit of flour to prevent sticking.
2. Combine Dry Ingredients
In a large mixing bowl, combine the whole wheat flour, all-purpose flour, baking soda, and salt.
3. Create a Well and Add Buttermilk
Make a well in the center of the dry ingredients and pour most of the buttermilk into it. Begin mixing with a wooden spoon or your hand until the dough comes together. Add more buttermilk if needed.
4. Knead and Shape

Turn the dough out onto a floured surface and knead it gently for about 1-2 minutes until it forms a round, flat loaf.

5. Score and Bake

Score a deep 'X' on the top of the loaf, place it on the prepared baking sheet, and bake at 425°F (220°C) for 15 minutes. Then, reduce the oven temperature to 400°F (200°C) and continue baking for 20-30 minutes, or until the bread is golden brown and sounds hollow when tapped on the bottom.

6. Cool and Serve

Allow the whole wheat soda bread to cool on a wire rack before slicing and serving. Enjoy it with your favorite spreads or as a hearty accompaniment to soups and stews.

Whole wheat soda bread combines the rustic charm of traditional Irish soda bread with the nutritional benefits of whole grains. Whether you opt for the classic whole wheat flour or experiment with different varieties, this bread is a nutritious and satisfying addition to your table.

Chapter 4: Rye Soda Bread

Hearty and Flavorful

Rye soda bread is a delightful departure from the traditional Irish soda bread made with wheat flour. Rye flour imparts a hearty and slightly earthy flavor, making it a popular choice for those who enjoy a more robust bread. In this chapter, we'll explore the world of rye soda bread, discover its unique characteristics, and learn about various rye flour options.

Characteristics of Rye Soda Bread

Rye soda bread offers distinct characteristics that set it apart from its wheat-based counterpart:

1. Flavor: Rye flour brings a rich, slightly nutty flavor to the bread, with hints of earthiness and sweetness. The flavor intensifies as the bread ages.

2. Texture: Rye soda bread has a denser texture compared to traditional white soda bread. It's hearty, moist, and perfect for sandwiches.

3. Nutritional Benefits: Rye flour is rich in dietary fiber, vitamins, and minerals. It provides a good source of nutrients such as magnesium, phosphorus, and B vitamins.

4. Gluten Content: Rye contains less gluten than wheat, which can make it a suitable option for those with mild gluten sensitivities. However, it's important to note that rye is not entirely gluten-free and may not be suitable for individuals with celiac disease.

Rye Flour Options

Before we delve into the recipe, let's explore the different rye flour options available:

1. Light Rye Flour: This type of rye flour is milled from the inner parts of the rye kernel, resulting in a lighter color and milder flavor. Light rye flour is often used for bread recipes where you want the rye flavor to be less pronounced.

2. Medium Rye Flour: Medium rye flour contains more of the bran and germ from the rye kernel, resulting in a slightly darker color and a stronger rye flavor. It's a popular choice for traditional rye bread recipes.

3. Dark Rye Flour: Dark rye flour is made from the whole rye kernel and has the most robust rye flavor. It's commonly used in traditional German and Scandinavian rye breads.

4. Pumpernickel Flour: Pumpernickel is an even darker and coarser rye flour. It's known for its deep, intense flavor and is often used in traditional pumpernickel bread recipes.

Rye Soda Bread Recipe
Ingredients:

- 1 1/2 cups rye flour (choose your preferred type)
- 1 1/2 cups all-purpose flour
- 1 teaspoon baking soda
- 1 teaspoon salt
- 1 1/2 cups buttermilk (approximately)

Instructions:

1. Preheat Your Oven

Preheat your oven to 425°F (220°C). Dust a baking sheet with a bit of flour to prevent sticking.

2. Combine Dry Ingredients

In a large mixing bowl, combine the rye flour (choose your preferred type), all-purpose flour, baking soda, and salt.

3. Make a Well and Add Buttermilk

Create a well in the center of the dry ingredients and pour most of the buttermilk into it. Begin mixing with a wooden spoon or your hand until the dough comes together. Add more buttermilk if needed.

4. Knead and Shape

Turn the dough out onto a floured surface and knead it gently for about 1-2 minutes until it forms a round, flat loaf.

5. Score and Bake

Score a deep 'X' on the top of the loaf, place it on the prepared baking sheet, and bake at 425°F (220°C) for 15 minutes. Then, reduce the oven temperature to 400°F (200°C) and continue baking for 20-30 minutes, or until the bread is golden brown and sounds hollow when tapped on the bottom.

6. Cool and Serve

Allow the rye soda bread to cool on a wire rack before slicing and serving. Enjoy it with your favorite spreads or use it to create delicious open-faced sandwiches.

Rye soda bread is a flavorful and hearty addition to your bread repertoire. Whether you prefer the milder taste of light rye or the robust flavor of dark rye, there's a rye soda bread variation to suit your palate.

Chapter 5: Gluten-Free Soda Bread

Suitable Flour Substitutes

For those with gluten sensitivities or celiac disease, enjoying traditional wheat-based soda bread can be a challenge. But fear not! Gluten-free soda bread offers a delicious alternative without compromising on taste or texture. In this chapter, we'll explore gluten-free flour substitutes suitable for soda bread and provide essential tips for baking a perfect gluten-free loaf.

Suitable Flour Substitutes

When making gluten-free soda bread, you'll need to replace traditional wheat flour with gluten-free alternatives. Here are some suitable options:

1. Gluten-Free All-Purpose Flour: You can find gluten-free all-purpose flour blends specifically formulated for baking. These blends typically contain a mix of rice flour, tapioca starch, and potato starch. They work well as a one-to-one substitute for regular wheat flour.

2. Rice Flour: Rice flour, whether white or brown, is a common gluten-free flour used in baking. It has a neutral flavor and is often used in combination with other flours to achieve the desired texture.

3. Oat Flour: Certified gluten-free oat flour is a versatile option. It adds a pleasant nutty flavor and a slightly chewy texture to your gluten-free soda bread.

4. Almond Flour: Almond flour, made from finely ground almonds, imparts a rich, slightly sweet flavor and a moist crumb. It's an excellent choice for those looking to add a nutty dimension to their bread.

5. Sorghum Flour: Sorghum flour is known for its mild flavor and fine texture, making it a good choice for gluten-free baking.

6. Buckwheat Flour: Despite the name, buckwheat is not related to wheat and is naturally gluten-free. It adds a hearty, earthy flavor to your soda bread.

7. Coconut Flour: Coconut flour is highly absorbent, so you'll need less of it compared to other flours. It offers a subtle coconut flavor and a unique texture.

Tips for a Perfect Gluten-Free Loaf

Baking gluten-free soda bread can be rewarding, but it also comes with some challenges. Here are essential tips to help you achieve a perfect gluten-free loaf:

1. Mix Different Flours: Consider using a blend of gluten-free flours to mimic the texture and taste of wheat-based soda bread. Experiment with different combinations to find the one you like best.

2. Add Xanthan Gum: Xanthan gum is a common gluten substitute that helps bind gluten-free flours together. Use it according to the package instructions to improve the texture of your bread.

3. Check the Liquid Ratio: Gluten-free flours may require more or less liquid than wheat flour. Adjust the amount of buttermilk or liquid called for in your recipe as needed to achieve the right dough consistency.

4. Let It Rest: Allow the gluten-free dough to rest for a few minutes before shaping and baking. This helps the flours absorb the liquid and improves the overall texture.

5. Be Gentle: Gluten-free dough can be fragile. Handle it gently when shaping the loaf to avoid making it tough or dense.

6. Preheat Your Oven: Ensure your oven is fully preheated to the specified temperature before baking the gluten-free soda bread. This helps with even baking and a nice crust formation.

7. Keep It Moist: Gluten-free bread tends to dry out faster than traditional bread. Store it in an airtight container or wrap it well to maintain its moisture.

Enjoy the satisfaction of baking gluten-free soda bread that's just as delicious and satisfying as its wheat-based counterpart. With the right flour substitutes and a few tips, you'll be creating gluten-free loaves that everyone can enjoy.

Chapter 6: Sweet Soda Bread Variations

Soda Bread Scones

Soda bread isn't just for savory occasions; it also shines in sweet variations. One delightful way to enjoy the sweetness of soda bread is by making soda bread scones. These scones are tender, slightly crumbly, and perfect for breakfast or as an afternoon treat with a cup of tea. In this section, we'll explore how to make soda bread scones that are sure to delight your taste buds.

Ingredients

For the Scones:

- 2 cups all-purpose flour
- 1/4 cup granulated sugar
- 1 teaspoon baking soda
- 1/2 teaspoon salt
- 4 tablespoons unsalted butter, cold and cubed
- 1 cup buttermilk
- 1/2 cup raisins or currants (optional)
- 1 teaspoon vanilla extract (optional)

For the Topping:

- 1 tablespoon buttermilk
- 1 tablespoon granulated sugar

Instructions

1. Preheat Your Oven

Preheat your oven to 425°F (220°C). Line a baking sheet with parchment paper or lightly grease it.

2. Combine Dry Ingredients

In a large mixing bowl, whisk together the all-purpose flour, granulated sugar, baking soda, and salt.

3. Add Cold Butter

Add the cold, cubed butter to the dry ingredients. Using a pastry cutter or your fingertips, work the butter into the flour mixture until it resembles coarse crumbs.

4. Incorporate Buttermilk

Pour in the buttermilk and, if desired, add the optional vanilla extract. Stir the mixture until it just comes together. Be careful not to overmix; a slightly shaggy dough is okay.

5. Add Raisins or Currants (Optional)

If you want to include raisins or currants for a sweet touch, gently fold them into the dough.

6. Shape and Cut

Turn the dough out onto a floured surface and pat it into a circle about 1-inch (2.5 cm) thick. Use a round cutter or a sharp knife to cut scones from the dough.

7. Brush with Buttermilk and Sugar

Place the scones on the prepared baking sheet. Brush the tops of the scones with buttermilk and sprinkle with granulated sugar for a beautiful golden finish.

8. Bake

Bake in the preheated oven for 15-20 minutes, or until the scones are golden brown and cooked through. They should sound hollow when tapped on the bottom.

9. Cool and Enjoy

Allow the soda bread scones to cool slightly on a wire rack before serving. Enjoy them warm with butter, jam, or clotted cream for a delightful treat.

Soda Bread with Dried Fruits

Adding dried fruits to soda bread is a wonderful way to infuse sweetness and a burst of flavor into this traditional bread. In this section we'll explore how to make soda bread with dried fruits, creating a delightful loaf that's perfect for breakfast or brunch.

Ingredients

For the Soda Bread:

- 2 cups all-purpose flour
- 2 tablespoons granulated sugar
- 1 teaspoon baking soda
- 1/2 teaspoon salt
- 4 tablespoons unsalted butter, cold and cubed
- 1 cup buttermilk
- 1/2 cup dried fruits (such as raisins, currants, or cranberries)
- 1 teaspoon vanilla extract (optional)

Instructions

1. Preheat Your Oven

Preheat your oven to 425°F (220°C). Line a baking sheet with parchment paper or lightly grease it.

2. Combine Dry Ingredients

In a large mixing bowl, whisk together the all-purpose flour, granulated sugar, baking soda, and salt.

3. Add Cold Butter

Add the cold, cubed butter to the dry ingredients. Using a pastry cutter or your fingertips, work the butter into the flour mixture until it resembles coarse crumbs.

4. Incorporate Buttermilk

Pour in the buttermilk and, if desired, add the optional vanilla extract. Stir the mixture until it just comes together. Be careful not to overmix; a slightly shaggy dough is okay.

5. Add Dried Fruits

Gently fold in the dried fruits of your choice into the dough until they are evenly distributed.

6. Shape and Bake

Turn the dough out onto a floured surface and shape it into a round loaf. Place the loaf on the prepared baking sheet.

7. Score the Top

Use a sharp knife to score a deep 'X' on the top of the loaf. This helps the bread bake evenly and creates an attractive design.

8. Bake

Bake in the preheated oven for 15-20 minutes, then reduce the oven temperature to 400°F (200°C) and continue baking for an additional 20-30 minutes, or until the bread is golden brown and sounds hollow when tapped on the bottom.

9. Cool and Enjoy

Allow the soda bread with dried fruits to cool on a wire rack before slicing and serving. It's wonderful when spread with butter or enjoyed as a sweet and satisfying snack.

Sweet soda bread variations like soda bread scones and soda bread with dried fruits add a touch of sweetness and flair to your baking repertoire. Whether you prefer the individual scone servings or a whole loaf, these recipes are sure to please your sweet tooth.

Chapter 7: Savory Soda Bread Twists

Cheesy Soda Bread

Cheese lovers, rejoice! Cheesy soda bread is a savory delight that combines the simplicity of traditional soda bread with the irresistible flavor of cheese. Whether served as a side dish, for breakfast, or as a snack, cheesy soda bread is sure to please. In this section, we'll explore how to make this flavorful variation.

Ingredients

For the Cheesy Soda Bread:

- 2 cups all-purpose flour
- 1 teaspoon baking soda
- 1 teaspoon salt
- 1 1/2 cups buttermilk
- 1 1/2 cups shredded cheese (cheddar, Gruyère, or your favorite melting cheese)
- 1/4 cup grated Parmesan cheese
- 2 tablespoons fresh chives, chopped
- 1/2 teaspoon garlic powder (optional)

Instructions

1. Preheat Your Oven

Preheat your oven to 425°F (220°C). Line a baking sheet with parchment paper or lightly grease it.

2. Combine Dry Ingredients

In a large mixing bowl, whisk together the all-purpose flour, baking soda, and salt.

3. Add Cheeses and Chives

Stir in the shredded cheese, grated Parmesan cheese, chopped fresh chives, and garlic powder (if using) into the dry ingredients.

4. Incorporate Buttermilk

Pour in the buttermilk and stir until all the ingredients are combined into a sticky dough.

5. Shape and Bake

Turn the dough out onto a floured surface and shape it into a round loaf. Place the loaf on the prepared baking sheet.

6. Score the Top

Use a sharp knife to score a deep 'X' on the top of the loaf. This helps the bread bake evenly and creates an attractive design.

7. Bake

Bake in the preheated oven for 15-20 minutes, then reduce the oven temperature to 400°F (200°C) and continue baking for an additional 20-30 minutes, or until the bread is golden brown and sounds hollow when tapped on the bottom.

8. Cool and Enjoy

Allow the cheesy soda bread to cool on a wire rack before slicing and serving. It's wonderful when served warm with a pat of butter or as a cheesy addition to soups and salads.

Herb and Garlic Soda Bread

Herb and garlic soda bread is a fragrant and savory variation that's perfect for enhancing your meals. The combination of fresh herbs and garlic creates a bread with a wonderful aroma and flavor. In this section, we'll explore how to make herb and garlic soda bread.

Ingredients

For the Herb and Garlic Soda Bread:

- 2 cups all-purpose flour
- 1 teaspoon baking soda
- 1 teaspoon salt
- 1 1/2 cups buttermilk
- 2 tablespoons fresh herbs (such as parsley, chives, or dill),

chopped

- 2 cloves garlic, minced
- 1/2 teaspoon dried oregano (optional)
- 1/2 teaspoon dried thyme (optional)

Instructions

1. Preheat Your Oven

Preheat your oven to 425°F (220°C). Line a baking sheet with parchment paper or lightly grease it.

2. Combine Dry Ingredients

In a large mixing bowl, whisk together the all-purpose flour, baking soda, and salt.

3. Add Fresh Herbs and Garlic

Stir in the chopped fresh herbs, minced garlic, and optional dried oregano and thyme into the dry ingredients.

4. Incorporate Buttermilk

Pour in the buttermilk and stir until all the ingredients are combined into a sticky dough.

5. Shape and Bake

Turn the dough out onto a floured surface and shape it into a round loaf. Place the loaf on the prepared baking sheet.

6. Score the Top

Use a sharp knife to score a deep 'X' on the top of the loaf. This helps the bread bake evenly and creates an attractive design.

7. Bake

Bake in the preheated oven for 15-20 minutes, then reduce the oven temperature to 400°F (200°C) and continue baking for an additional 20-30 minutes, or until the bread is golden brown and sounds hollow when tapped on the bottom.

8. Cool and Enjoy

Allow the herb and garlic soda bread to cool on a wire rack before slicing and serving. It's delicious alongside your favorite soups, salads, or as a flavorful accompaniment to a cheese platter.

Savory soda bread twists like cheesy soda bread and herb and garlic soda bread add a burst of flavor and aroma to your baking repertoire. Whether you're a cheese enthusiast or a fan of fresh herbs and garlic, these recipes offer a savory treat for your taste buds.

Chapter 8: Sourdough Soda Bread

Combining Two Traditions

Sourdough soda bread is a delightful fusion of two beloved bread-making traditions: the tangy and complex flavors of sourdough and the simplicity of soda bread. This unique bread offers a tender crumb and the distinct taste of sourdough, making it a favorite among bread enthusiasts. In this section, we'll explore how to create sourdough soda bread by combining the best of both worlds.

Sourdough Starter Guide

Before we dive into the sourdough soda bread recipe, let's start with a guide on creating and maintaining a sourdough starter:

Creating a Sourdough Starter:

To make your own sourdough starter, follow these steps:

Ingredients:

- 1 cup all-purpose flour
- 1/2 cup lukewarm water

Instructions:

Day 1: In a glass or plastic container, combine 1/2 cup of all-purpose flour with 1/4 cup of lukewarm water. Mix until you have a thick paste. Cover loosely and let it sit at room temperature for 24 hours.

Day 2: You may not see much activity, but that's okay. Discard half of the mixture and add another 1/2 cup of all-purpose flour and 1/4 cup of lukewarm water. Mix well, cover, and let it rest for another 24 hours.

Day 3 and Beyond: You should start to see bubbles and notice a sour smell. Continue the feeding process by discarding half of the mixture and adding 1/2 cup of all-purpose flour and 1/4 cup of lukewarm water daily. After a few days, your starter should be active and ready for baking.

Maintaining Your Sourdough Starter:

Keep your sourdough starter in a glass or plastic container with a loose lid or cover it with a cloth.

Store it at room temperature or in the refrigerator, depending on how often you plan to bake. Refrigerated starters require less frequent feeding.

To maintain your starter's activity, feed it once a week by discarding half and adding equal parts of all-purpose flour and water.

Now, let's proceed with the sourdough soda bread recipe.

Sourdough Soda Bread Recipe

Ingredients:

- 2 cups all-purpose flour
- 1 teaspoon baking soda
- 1 teaspoon salt
- 1 cup active sourdough starter
- 1/2 cup buttermilk (approximately)

Instructions:

1. Preheat Your Oven

Preheat your oven to 425°F (220°C). Dust a baking sheet with a bit of flour to prevent sticking.

2. Combine Dry Ingredients

In a large mixing bowl, whisk together the all-purpose flour, baking soda, and salt.

3. Add Sourdough Starter

Add the active sourdough starter to the dry ingredients and mix well. The sourdough starter provides leavening and imparts its signature tangy flavor.

4. Incorporate Buttermilk

Pour in the buttermilk and stir until all the ingredients come together into a sticky dough. You may need to adjust the amount of buttermilk slightly based on the hydration of your sourdough starter.

5. Shape and Bake

Turn the dough out onto a floured surface and shape it into a round loaf. Place the loaf on the prepared baking sheet.

6. Score the Top

Use a sharp knife to score a deep 'X' on the top of the loaf. This helps the bread bake evenly and creates an attractive design.

7. Bake

Bake in the preheated oven for 15-20 minutes, then reduce the oven temperature to 400°F (200°C) and continue baking for an additional 20-30 minutes, or until the bread is golden brown and sounds hollow when tapped on the bottom.

8. Cool and Enjoy

Allow the sourdough soda bread to cool on a wire rack before slicing and serving. The tangy flavor of the sourdough complements the simplicity of soda bread, creating a delightful combination.

Sourdough soda bread brings together the best of both worlds: the rich flavor and aroma of sourdough and the quick and easy preparation of soda bread. It's a fantastic bread to enjoy as a standalone treat or alongside your favorite dishes.

Chapter 9: Stuffed Soda Breads

Cheesy Stuffed Bread

Cheesy stuffed soda bread is a delightful twist on traditional soda bread. Imagine a golden-brown loaf with a surprise inside: a molten, cheesy center that oozes with flavor. It's the perfect accompaniment to soups, a savory snack, or a delicious addition to your next meal. In this section, we'll explore how to create a cheesy stuffed soda bread that will leave your taste buds craving for more.

Ingredients

For the Cheesy Stuffed Bread:

- 3 cups all-purpose flour
- 1 teaspoon baking soda
- 1 teaspoon salt
- 1 1/2 cups buttermilk
- 1 1/2 cups shredded cheese (cheddar, mozzarella, or your favorite melting cheese)
- 1/4 cup grated Parmesan cheese
- 1/4 cup chopped fresh herbs (such as parsley, chives, or thyme)
- 1/2 teaspoon garlic powder (optional)

For the Filling:

- 1 1/2 cups shredded cheese (same type as above)
- Additional chopped fresh herbs for garnish

Instructions

1. Preheat Your Oven

Preheat your oven to 425°F (220°C). Line a baking sheet with parchment paper or lightly grease it.

2. Combine Dry Ingredients

In a large mixing bowl, whisk together the all-purpose flour, baking soda, and salt.

3. Add Herbs, Parmesan, and Optional Garlic Powder

Stir in the chopped fresh herbs, grated Parmesan cheese, and optional garlic powder into the dry ingredients.

4. Incorporate Buttermilk

Pour in the buttermilk and stir until all the ingredients come together into a sticky dough.

5. Shape the Dough

Turn the dough out onto a floured surface and divide it in half. Flatten one half into a round disc, approximately 1 inch (2.5 cm) thick.

6. Add the Cheese Filling

Sprinkle half of the shredded cheese for the filling over the flattened dough, leaving a border around the edges. You want to create a layer of cheese in the center.

7. Encase the Cheese

Take the remaining half of the dough and flatten it into a disc of similar size. Carefully place it over the cheese-covered dough and press the edges to seal. It should resemble a sandwich with cheese inside.

8. Shape and Score

Shape the stuffed dough into a round loaf and place it on the prepared baking sheet. Use a sharp knife to score a deep 'X' on the top of the loaf.

9. Bake

Bake in the preheated oven for 15-20 minutes, then reduce the oven temperature to 400°F (200°C) and continue baking for an additional 20-30 minutes, or until the bread is golden brown and sounds hollow when tapped on the bottom.

10. Cool and Garnish

Allow the cheesy stuffed bread to cool on a wire rack. Once cooled, garnish with additional chopped fresh herbs for a vibrant finish.

Cheesy stuffed soda bread is a delicious blend of textures and flavors, with the warmth of freshly baked bread and the gooey goodness of melted cheese in every bite.

Savory Filling Ideas

Savory stuffed soda breads open up a world of possibilities for creating unique and flavorful loaves. Whether you're looking to add a savory twist to your bread or want a hearty snack, these filling ideas are sure to inspire your culinary creativity. Here are some savory filling ideas to get you started:

1. Spinach and Feta:

Sautéed spinach with garlic and onions, mixed with crumbled feta cheese.

2. Sun-Dried Tomato and Basil:

Chopped sun-dried tomatoes, fresh basil leaves, and grated Parmesan cheese.

3. Caramelized Onion and Gruyere:

Slow-cooked caramelized onions and grated Gruyere cheese for a sweet and savory combination.

4. Pepperoni and Mozzarella:

Sliced pepperoni and shredded mozzarella cheese for a pizza-inspired filling.

5. Mushroom and Swiss:

Sautéed mushrooms with garlic and Swiss cheese.

6. Bacon and Cheddar:

Crispy bacon bits and shredded cheddar cheese for a smoky flavor.

7. Pesto and Goat Cheese:

Pesto sauce and crumbled goat cheese for a burst of herbaceous Ness.

Feel free to experiment with different combinations to create the perfect savory stuffed soda bread that suits your taste. The possibilities are endless, and your guests will love the surprise of a flavorful filling inside each slice.

Chapter 10: Flavored Soda Bread Spreads

Homemade Butter

Flavored spreads elevate the enjoyment of soda bread, and homemade butter is a true delight. Making your own butter allows you to infuse it with various flavors, creating a personalized condiment for your freshly baked soda bread. In this section, we'll explore how to prepare homemade flavored butter to enhance the taste of your soda bread.

Basic Homemade Butter Recipe

Ingredients:

- 1 cup heavy cream
- Pinch of salt (optional)
- Ice water (for rinsing)

Instructions:

1. Whip the Cream

Pour the heavy cream into a food processor or stand mixer fitted with a whisk attachment. Add a pinch of salt if desired for flavor. Whip the cream on medium-high speed until it thickens and the consistency changes from whipped cream to butter.

2. Separate the Butter

Continue whipping until the fat separates from the liquid. This can take several minutes. You'll notice small clumps forming.

3. Drain and Rinse

Once the butterfat has separated, drain off the liquid (buttermilk) and reserve it for later use. Place the butter in a bowl.

4. Rinse the Butter

To remove any remaining buttermilk, rinse the butter by adding ice water to the bowl. Gently knead the butter in the cold water, then pour off the water and repeat until the water runs clear. This helps prolong the shelf life of the butter.

5. Flavor the Butter

At this stage, you can add flavorings to your butter. Here are some ideas:

Herb Butter: Mix in finely chopped fresh herbs like parsley, chives, or dill.

Garlic Butter: Add minced garlic for a savory, aromatic spread.

Honey Butter: Drizzle in honey and a pinch of cinnamon for a sweet, honey-infused butter.

Spiced Butter: Incorporate your favorite spices or seasonings, such as paprika, cayenne pepper, or smoked salt.

Lemon Butter: Grate lemon zest and squeeze in lemon juice for a zesty, citrusy flavor.

6. Shape and Store

Shape the flavored butter into a log or place it in a small dish. Wrap it tightly in plastic wrap or parchment paper and refrigerate. The butter can also be frozen for longer storage.

Enjoy your homemade flavored butter with freshly baked soda bread!

Jam and Jelly Complements

Soda bread pairs wonderfully with a variety of jams, jellies, and preserves. These sweet spreads add a burst of fruity flavor and sweetness to the bread, creating a delightful contrast. In this section, we'll explore some classic and creative jam and jelly complements for your soda bread.

Classic Combinations:

Irish Soda Bread with Raspberry Jam: The tartness of raspberry jam complements the simplicity of Irish soda bread beautifully.

Orange Marmalade on Whole Wheat Soda Bread: The zesty bitterness of orange marmalade pairs well with the nutty flavors of whole wheat soda bread.

Blackberry Jam on White Soda Bread: The rich sweetness of blackberry jam enhances the mild taste of white soda bread.

Creative Combinations:

Fig Preserves on Rye Soda Bread: The earthy sweetness of fig preserves complements the hearty and flavorful rye soda bread.

Spiced Pear Jam on Sweet Soda Bread: Spiced pear jam adds warm and comforting flavors to sweet soda bread variations.

Blueberry Compote on Cheesy Soda Bread: Blueberry compote offers a sweet-tart contrast to the savory cheesiness of stuffed soda bread.

Feel free to explore different flavor combinations to discover your favorite jam and jelly complements for soda bread. With a variety of options available, you can customize your soda bread experience to suit your taste.

Chapter 11: International Soda Bread Recipes

American Buttermilk Biscuits

American Buttermilk Biscuits are a classic treat that embodies the heartiness and simplicity of soda bread. These biscuits are tender, flaky, and perfect for breakfast, as a side dish, or as a complement to various dishes. In this section, we'll explore how to make American Buttermilk Biscuits, a beloved staple in American cuisine.

Ingredients

For the Buttermilk Biscuits:

- 2 cups all-purpose flour
- 2 1/2 teaspoons baking powder
- 1/2 teaspoon baking soda
- 1 teaspoon salt
- 1/2 cup unsalted butter, cold and cubed
- 3/4 cup buttermilk

Instructions

1. Preheat Your Oven

Preheat your oven to 450°F (230°C). Line a baking sheet with parchment paper or lightly grease it.

2. Combine Dry Ingredients

In a large mixing bowl, whisk together the all-purpose flour, baking powder, baking soda, and salt.

3. Add Cold Butter

Add the cold, cubed butter to the dry ingredients. Using a pastry cutter or your fingertips, work the butter into the flour mixture until it resembles coarse crumbs.

4. Incorporate Buttermilk

Pour in the buttermilk and stir until the mixture comes together into a sticky dough. Be careful not to overmix; a slightly shaggy dough is okay.

5. Shape and Cut

Turn the dough out onto a floured surface and pat it into a rectangle, about 1-inch (2.5 cm) thick. Use a round cutter or a sharp knife to cut out biscuits from the dough.

6. Bake

Place the biscuits on the prepared baking sheet, spacing them about 1 inch apart. Bake in the preheated oven for 10-12 minutes, or until the biscuits are golden brown and cooked through.

7. Cool and Enjoy

Allow the American Buttermilk Biscuits to cool slightly on a wire rack before serving. These biscuits are wonderful when served with butter, gravy, or jam.

Australian Damper

Australian Damper is a traditional Australian bush bread that shares similarities with soda bread. It's simple, rustic, and has a delightful crust that's perfect for tearing apart and sharing around a campfire. In this section, we'll explore how to make Australian Damper, a beloved staple in Australian cuisine.

Ingredients
For the Australian Damper:

- 3 cups self-raising flour
- Pinch of salt
- 1 1/4 cups water

Instructions

1. Preheat Your Oven or Prepare a Campfire

If you're making damper indoors, preheat your oven to 425°F (220°C). If you're making it outdoors, prepare a campfire and let it burn down to hot coals.

2. Combine Dry Ingredients

In a large mixing bowl, combine the self-raising flour and a pinch of salt.

3. Add Water

Gradually add the water to the dry ingredients, mixing with a wooden spoon or your hands until the dough comes together.

4. Knead the Dough

Turn the dough out onto a floured surface and knead it lightly for a few minutes until it's smooth and elastic.

5. Shape the Damper

Shape the dough into a round loaf, about 1 inch (2.5 cm) thick.

6. Bake or Cook Over Coals

If using an oven, place the damper on a baking sheet and bake for 25-30 minutes or until it's golden brown and sounds hollow when tapped on the bottom. If cooking over coals, wrap the damper in foil and place it in the hot coals, turning occasionally for about 20-25 minutes, or until it's cooked through.

7. Cool and Enjoy

Allow the Australian Damper to cool slightly before tearing it apart and serving. It's delicious when served with butter, golden syrup, or jam.

American Buttermilk Biscuits and Australian Damper are classic examples of soda bread variations from around the world. Whether you're enjoying the flaky, buttery biscuits of America or the rustic simplicity of Australian Damper, these recipes offer a taste of international soda bread traditions.

Chapter 12: Soda Bread in a Pinch

Emergency Soda Bread

Emergency soda bread is your go-to recipe when you need fresh bread in a hurry. With minimal ingredients and a short preparation time, you can have a warm loaf of soda bread on the table in no time. Whether unexpected guests arrive or you simply crave a quick bread fix, this recipe has got you covered.

Ingredients

For the Emergency Soda Bread:

- 2 cups all-purpose flour
- 1 teaspoon baking soda
- 1/2 teaspoon salt
- 1 cup buttermilk

Instructions

1. Preheat Your Oven

Preheat your oven to 425°F (220°C). Line a baking sheet with parchment paper or lightly grease it.

2. Combine Dry Ingredients

In a large mixing bowl, whisk together the all-purpose flour, baking soda, and salt.

3. Incorporate Buttermilk

Pour in the buttermilk and stir until the mixture comes together into a sticky dough.

4. Shape and Cut

Turn the dough out onto a floured surface and shape it into a round loaf, about 1 inch (2.5 cm) thick. Use a sharp knife to score a deep 'X' on the top of the loaf. This helps the bread bake evenly and creates an attractive design.

5. Bake

Place the loaf on the prepared baking sheet and bake in the preheated oven for 15-20 minutes, then reduce the oven temperature to 400°F (200°C) and continue baking for an additional 20-30 minutes, or until the bread is golden brown and sounds hollow when tapped on the bottom.

6. Cool and Enjoy

Allow the emergency soda bread to cool slightly on a wire rack before serving. It's perfect when served warm with butter or jam. This quick and easy recipe is a lifesaver when you need freshly baked bread on short notice.

Quick and Easy Recipes

Life can be busy, but that doesn't mean you have to sacrifice the joy of freshly baked soda bread. In this section, we'll explore a few quick and easy soda bread recipes that can be prepared with minimal effort and time. These recipes are perfect for those moments when you want to enjoy homemade bread without a lengthy preparation process.

1. Three-Ingredient Soda Bread:
Ingredients:

- 2 cups self-raising flour
- 1/2 teaspoon salt
- 1 cup buttermilk

Instructions:

1. Combine the self-raising flour and salt in a bowl.

1. Stir in the buttermilk until a sticky dough forms.

1. Shape into a round loaf, score the top, and bake at 425°F (220°C) for 15-20 minutes, then at 400°F (200°C) for 20-30

minutes until golden brown.

2. Quick Whole Wheat Soda Bread:
Ingredients:

- 2 cups whole wheat flour
- 1 teaspoon baking soda
- 1/2 teaspoon salt
- 1 cup buttermilk

Instructions:

1. Combine the whole wheat flour, baking soda, and salt in a bowl.

1. Stir in the buttermilk until a sticky dough forms.

1. Shape into a round loaf, score the top, and bake as directed above.

3. Fast Rye Soda Bread:
Ingredients:

- 1 cup rye flour
- 1 cup all-purpose flour
- 1 teaspoon baking soda
- 1/2 teaspoon salt
- 1 cup buttermilk

Instructions:

1. Combine the rye flour, all-purpose flour, baking soda, and salt in a bowl.

1. Stir in the buttermilk until a sticky dough forms.

1. Shape into a round loaf, score the top, and bake as directed above.

These quick and easy soda bread recipes ensure that you can enjoy homemade bread without sacrificing precious time.

Chapter 13: Soda Bread for Special Occasions

Holiday Variations

Soda bread isn't just for everyday meals; it can also be a special treat during holidays and celebrations. Whether you're celebrating St. Patrick's Day, Thanksgiving, or any other special occasion, these holiday variations of soda bread will add a festive touch to your table. In this section, we'll explore some delightful holiday soda bread recipes.

St. Patrick's Day Soda Bread:

Ingredients:

- 3 cups all-purpose flour
- 1 teaspoon baking soda
- 1 teaspoon salt
- 1 1/2 cups buttermilk
- 1/2 cup raisins or currants
- 1/4 cup caraway seeds (optional)

Instructions:

1. Preheat your oven to 425°F (220°C). Line a baking sheet with parchment paper or lightly grease it.

1. In a large mixing bowl, whisk together the all-purpose flour, baking soda, and salt.

1. Stir in the buttermilk, raisins or currants, and caraway seeds (if using) until the mixture forms a sticky dough.

1. Shape the dough into a round loaf, score the top with a deep 'X,' and bake as directed in previous recipes.

Thanksgiving Soda Bread with Cranberries and Nuts:
Ingredients:

- 2 cups all-purpose flour
- 1 teaspoon baking soda
- 1/2 teaspoon salt
- 1 1/2 cups buttermilk
- 1/2 cup dried cranberries
- 1/2 cup chopped nuts (such as pecans or walnuts)

Instructions:

1. Preheat your oven to 425°F (220°C). Line a baking sheet with parchment paper or lightly grease it.

1. In a large mixing bowl, whisk together the all-purpose flour, baking soda, and salt.
2. Stir in the buttermilk, dried cranberries, and chopped nuts until the mixture forms a sticky dough.

1. Shape the dough into a round loaf, score the top with a deep 'X, and bake as directed in previous recipes.

These holiday soda bread variations are perfect for adding a special touch to your festive meals.

Soda Bread Stuffing

Soda bread stuffing is a delightful alternative to traditional bread stuffing. Its hearty texture and unique flavor add a twist to your holiday meals. Whether you're stuffing a turkey, chicken, or serving it as a side dish, soda bread stuffing is sure to be a crowd-pleaser. In this section, we'll explore how to make soda bread stuffing.

Ingredients:

- 8 cups cubed soda bread (any variety)

- 1/2 cup unsalted butter
- 1 large onion, finely chopped
- 2 celery stalks, finely chopped
- 2 cloves garlic, minced
- 2 teaspoons dried sage (or 2 tablespoons fresh sage, chopped)
- 1 teaspoon dried thyme (or 1 tablespoon fresh thyme leaves)
- 1 teaspoon salt
- 1/2 teaspoon black pepper
- 2 1/2 cups chicken or vegetable broth
- 1/2 cup dried cranberries or raisins (optional)
- Chopped fresh parsley for garnish

Instructions:

1. Prepare the Soda Bread Cubes

Cut your soda bread into 1-inch (2.5 cm) cubes and spread them out on a baking sheet to dry overnight. Alternatively, you can toast them in the oven at 300°F (150°C) for about 15-20 minutes until they're slightly crispy.

2. Sauté the Vegetables

In a large skillet or frying pan, melt the unsalted butter over medium heat. Add the finely chopped onion and celery and sauté until they become soft and translucent, about 5-7 minutes. Stir in the minced garlic, dried sage, dried thyme, salt, and black pepper, and cook for an additional 2 minutes until fragrant.

3. Mix Ingredients

In a large mixing bowl, combine the cubed soda bread and the sautéed vegetable mixture. If desired, add the dried cranberries or raisins for a touch of sweetness.

4. Add Broth

Pour the chicken or vegetable broth over the bread and vegetable mixture. Gently toss to combine until the liquid is evenly absorbed. If the mixture seems too dry, you can add a bit more broth.

5. Bake

Transfer the stuffing mixture to a greased baking dish. Cover it with foil and bake in a preheated oven at 350°F (175°C) for 30 minutes. Then, remove the foil and bake for an additional 15-20 minutes or until the top is golden brown and crispy.

6. Garnish and Serve

Once out of the oven, garnish the soda bread stuffing with chopped fresh parsley for a burst of color and freshness. Serve it as a side dish or use it to stuff your holiday poultry.

Soda bread stuffing is a unique and flavorful addition to your holiday feasts, adding a touch of Irish tradition to your table.

Chapter 14: Baking with Soda Bread Crumbs

Breadcrumbs and Coatings

Soda bread crumbs are a versatile ingredient that can be used in various ways in the kitchen. They add texture and flavor to a wide range of dishes, from coating fried foods to creating a crispy topping for casseroles. In this section, we'll explore how to make and use soda bread crumbs as breadcrumbs and coatings for your culinary creations.

Making Soda Bread Crumbs:

Ingredients:

- Stale soda bread slices

Instructions:

1. Allow your soda bread to become slightly stale. Fresh bread will not produce the desired texture for breadcrumbs.

1. Cut or tear the stale soda bread into small pieces or cubes.

1. Place the bread pieces on a baking sheet and let them air dry for a few hours or overnight. Alternatively, you can use an oven to dry them more quickly. Preheat the oven to 300°F (150°C), spread the bread pieces on a baking sheet, and bake for about 10-15 minutes until they become crisp and dry but not browned.

1. Once the bread pieces are completely dry, use a food processor or a blender to pulse them into fine crumbs. You now have homemade soda bread crumbs ready for various culinary uses.

Coating and Breading with Soda Bread Crumbs:

Soda bread crumbs make an excellent coating for a variety of dishes. Here are some ideas:

1. Breaded Chicken or Fish:

Dip chicken breasts or fish fillets into beaten eggs, then coat them with soda bread crumbs seasoned with salt, pepper, and herbs. Pan-fry or bake until crispy and golden brown.

2. Vegetable Schnitzel:

Coat sliced eggplant, zucchini, or portobello mushrooms with soda bread crumbs, then pan-fry until crispy. Serve with your favorite dipping sauce.

3. Stuffed Mushrooms:

Prepare a stuffing mixture of breadcrumbs, herbs, cheese, and minced mushrooms. Fill mushroom caps with the mixture, top with soda bread crumbs, and bake until golden and bubbling.

4. Onion Rings:

Dip onion rings into a batter of flour, milk, and spices, then coat them with soda bread crumbs before deep frying until crisp and golden.

5. Mozzarella Sticks:

Cut mozzarella cheese into sticks, dip them in beaten egg, coat with soda bread crumbs, and deep-fry until the cheese is melty and the coating is crispy.

Topping Ideas:

Soda bread crumbs can also be used as toppings for various dishes:

1. Macaroni and Cheese:

Sprinkle soda bread crumbs mixed with melted butter and grated Parmesan cheese over your baked macaroni and cheese for a crunchy, cheesy topping.

2. Casseroles:

Add a layer of soda bread crumbs mixed with herbs and butter on top of casseroles before baking. It creates a crispy and flavorful topping.

3. Vegetable Gratin:

Top roasted or steamed vegetables with a mixture of soda bread crumbs, grated cheese, and herbs. Bake until bubbly and golden.

4. Baked Pasta:

Make a crispy topping for baked pasta dishes by combining soda bread crumbs with melted butter, garlic, and grated cheese.

Soda bread crumbs are a versatile and budget-friendly ingredient that can elevate your dishes with added crunch and flavor. Experiment with different seasonings and recipes to discover new and exciting ways to use them in your cooking.

Chapter 15: Creative Leftover Soda Bread Recipes

Croutons and Salad Toppings

Leftover soda bread can be transformed into delicious croutons and salad toppings that add a delightful crunch to your salads and soups. Making croutons from soda bread is not only a clever way to repurpose leftovers but also a tasty way to elevate your dishes. In this section, we'll explore how to make soda bread croutons and salad toppings.

Ingredients:

- Leftover soda bread (white or whole wheat)
- Olive oil or melted butter
- Salt and pepper
- Optional seasonings (garlic powder, dried herbs, grated Parmesan cheese, etc.)

Instructions:

1. Prepare the Bread:

Cut your leftover soda bread into small cubes. The size of the cubes can vary based on your preference, but typically, 1/2 to 1-inch (1 to 2.5 cm) cubes work well.

2. Season the Croutons:

Place the bread cubes in a mixing bowl. Drizzle them with olive oil or melted butter, just enough to coat them lightly. Season with salt, pepper, and any optional seasonings you like. Toss the cubes to ensure they're evenly coated.

3. Bake the Croutons:

Spread the seasoned bread cubes in a single layer on a baking sheet. Bake in a preheated oven at 375°F (190°C) for about 10-15 minutes, or until the croutons are golden brown and crispy. Keep a close eye on them to prevent burning, as baking times can vary.

4. Cool and Store:

Once the croutons are done, remove them from the oven and let them cool completely. Store them in an airtight container for later use.

5. Salad Toppings:

Sprinkle your homemade soda bread croutons on salads just before serving. They add a delightful crunch and a unique flavor that store-bought croutons can't match.

Soup Garnish:

Float soda bread croutons on top of your favorite soups for added texture and flavor. They work particularly well with creamy soups like tomato bisque or potato leek.

Bread Pudding

Soda bread is an excellent base for creating a flavorful and comforting bread pudding. Whether you have leftover soda bread or simply want to enjoy this classic dessert, soda bread bread pudding is a delightful treat. In this section, we'll explore how to make soda bread pudding.

Ingredients:

- 4 cups cubed stale soda bread (any variety)
- 2 cups milk
- 2 large eggs
- 1/2 cup granulated sugar
- 1 teaspoon vanilla extract
- 1/2 teaspoon ground cinnamon (optional)
- 1/4 cup raisins or currants (optional)
- Butter or cooking spray for greasing the baking dish

Instructions:

1. Prepare the Bread:

Cut your stale soda bread into 1-inch (2.5 cm) cubes.

2. Preheat the Oven:

Preheat your oven to 350°F (175°C). Grease a baking dish with butter or cooking spray.

3. Create the Custard Mixture:

In a mixing bowl, whisk together the milk, eggs, granulated sugar, vanilla extract, and ground cinnamon (if using). Whisk until well combined.

4. Assemble the Pudding:

Place half of the cubed soda bread in the greased baking dish. Sprinkle with half of the raisins or currants (if using). Add the remaining soda bread cubes and top with the remaining raisins or currants.

5. Pour the Custard:

Slowly pour the custard mixture over the bread, ensuring all the bread is soaked. Press down on the bread cubes with a fork or spatula to help them absorb the custard.

6. Bake the Pudding:

Place the baking dish in the preheated oven and bake for 45-55 minutes, or until the pudding is set and the top is golden brown.

7. Serve Warm:

Allow the soda bread pudding to cool slightly before serving. It's delicious on its own or with a drizzle of custard sauce or a scoop of vanilla ice cream.

Soda bread pudding is a comforting and delightful dessert that transforms leftovers into something special.

Chapter 16: Gluten-Free and Vegan Soda Bread

Allergen-Free Options

Gluten-free and vegan soda bread allows those with dietary restrictions or preferences to enjoy the classic flavors and texture of soda bread. Whether you have celiac disease, gluten sensitivity, or follow a plant-based diet, these recipes provide delicious alternatives without compromising on taste. In this section, we'll explore how to make gluten-free and vegan soda bread with allergen-free options.

Gluten-Free Soda Bread:

Ingredients:

- 2 cups gluten-free all-purpose flour (with xanthan gum)
- 1 teaspoon baking soda
- 1/2 teaspoon salt
- 1 1/2 cups dairy-free buttermilk (made with non-dairy milk and lemon juice or vinegar)
- 1/2 cup raisins or currants (optional)

Instructions:

1. Preheat your oven to 425°F (220°C). Line a baking sheet with parchment paper or lightly grease it.

1. In a large mixing bowl, whisk together the gluten-free all-purpose flour, baking soda, and salt.

1. If using raisins or currants, fold them into the dry ingredients.

1. Pour the dairy-free buttermilk into the dry ingredients and stir until the mixture comes together into a sticky dough.

1. Shape the dough into a round loaf, score the top with a deep 'X,' and place it on the prepared baking sheet.

1. Bake in the preheated oven for 15-20 minutes, then reduce the oven temperature to 400°F (200°C) and continue baking for an additional 20-30 minutes, or until the bread is golden brown and sounds hollow when tapped on the bottom.

1. Allow the gluten-free soda bread to cool slightly on a wire rack before serving.

Vegan Soda Bread:
Ingredients:

- 3 cups all-purpose flour
- 1 teaspoon baking soda
- 1/2 teaspoon salt
- 1 1/2 cups dairy-free buttermilk (made with non-dairy milk and lemon juice or vinegar)
- 1/4 cup vegetable oil or melted coconut oil
- 1/4 cup sugar (optional)
- 1/2 cup raisins or currants (optional)

Instructions:

1. Preheat your oven to 425°F (220°C). Line a baking sheet with parchment paper or lightly grease it.

1. In a large mixing bowl, whisk together the all-purpose flour, baking soda, and salt.

1. If using sugar, fold it into the dry ingredients.

1. If using raisins or currants, fold them into the dry ingredients.

1. Pour the dairy-free buttermilk and vegetable oil into the dry ingredients and stir until the mixture comes together into a sticky dough.

1. Shape the dough into a round loaf, score the top with a deep 'X' and place it on the prepared baking sheet.

1. Bake in the preheated oven for 15-20 minutes, then reduce the oven temperature to 400°F (200°C) and continue baking for an additional 20-30 minutes, or until the bread is golden brown and sounds hollow when tapped on the bottom.

1. Allow the vegan soda bread to cool slightly on a wire rack before serving.

These allergen-free options for gluten-free and vegan soda bread ensure that everyone can enjoy this classic bread, regardless of dietary restrictions or preferences.

Plant-Based Substitutes

Plant-based substitutes in soda bread recipes offer a compassionate and environmentally friendly twist on this traditional bread. By using dairy-free buttermilk and plant-based fats, you can create delicious vegan soda bread while reducing your carbon footprint. In this section, we'll explore how to make soda bread with plant-based substitutes.

Ingredients:

- 3 cups all-purpose flour
- 1 teaspoon baking soda
- 1/2 teaspoon salt
- 1 1/2 cups dairy-free buttermilk (made with non-dairy milk and lemon juice or vinegar)
- 1/4 cup vegetable oil or melted coconut oil
- 1/4 cup sugar (optional)

- 1/2 cup raisins or currants (optional)

Instructions:

1. Preheat your oven to 425°F (220°C). Line a baking sheet with parchment paper or lightly grease it.

1. In a large mixing bowl, whisk together the all-purpose flour, baking soda, and salt.

1. If using sugar, fold it into the dry ingredients.

1. If using raisins or currants, fold them into the dry ingredients.

1. Pour the dairy-free buttermilk and vegetable oil into the dry ingredients and stir until the mixture comes together into a sticky dough.

1. Shape the dough into a round loaf, score the top with a deep 'X,' and place it on the prepared baking sheet.

1. Bake in the preheated oven for 15-20 minutes, then reduce the oven temperature to 400°F (200°C) and continue baking for an additional 20-30 minutes, or until the bread is golden brown and sounds hollow when tapped on the bottom.

1. Allow the plant-based soda bread to cool slightly on a wire rack before serving.

Plant-based substitutes in soda bread recipes allow you to enjoy this classic bread while making eco-conscious choices.

Chapter 17: Soda Bread for Beginners

Step-by-Step Basics

Soda bread is a perfect choice for beginners in the world of bread baking. It's quick, easy, and doesn't require yeast or extensive kneading. In this section, we'll walk you through the step-by-step basics of making soda bread, ensuring your journey into baking is a delightful one.

Ingredients for Classic White Soda Bread:

- 3 cups all-purpose flour
- 1 teaspoon baking soda
- 1 teaspoon salt
- 1 1/2 cups buttermilk

Instructions:

1. Preheat Your Oven:

Preheat your oven to 425°F (220°C). While the oven is preheating, place a cast-iron skillet or a baking sheet in the oven to heat.

2. Mix Dry Ingredients:

In a large mixing bowl, whisk together the all-purpose flour, baking soda, and salt.

3. Add Buttermilk:

Make a well in the center of the dry ingredients and pour in most of the buttermilk. Reserve a small amount to adjust the dough consistency later. Using a wooden spoon or your hands, mix the ingredients until they come together to form a sticky dough.

4. Knead Lightly:

Turn the dough out onto a lightly floured surface. Knead it gently for a few seconds until it's smoother but still slightly sticky. Avoid over-kneading, as soda bread doesn't require extensive kneading like yeast breads.

5. Shape and Score:

Form the dough into a round loaf, about 1 inch (2.5 cm) thick. Place the dough on a piece of parchment paper dusted with flour. Use a sharp knife to score a deep 'X' on the top of the loaf. This helps the bread bake evenly.

6. Bake:

Carefully remove the preheated skillet or baking sheet from the oven. Transfer the parchment paper with the soda bread onto the hot skillet or baking sheet. Bake in the preheated oven for 15-20 minutes, then reduce the oven temperature to 400°F (200°C) and continue baking for an additional 20-30 minutes, or until the bread is golden brown and sounds hollow when tapped on the bottom.

7. Cool and Enjoy:

Allow the soda bread to cool slightly on a wire rack before slicing and serving. It's best enjoyed fresh and warm with butter.

Troubleshooting Tips

Common Issues and How to Fix Them

Dough Too Dry: If your dough is too dry and crumbly, gradually add the reserved buttermilk or a bit of water, a tablespoon at a time, until the dough comes together.

Dough Too Sticky: If your dough is excessively sticky and hard to handle, add a little more flour, a tablespoon at a time, until it's manageable.

Over-Kneading: Avoid over-kneading the dough, as it can lead to a tough loaf. Knead only until it's smooth.

Bread Browning Too Quickly: If the bread is browning too quickly in the oven, tent it with aluminum foil to prevent over-browning while allowing it to continue baking.

Bread Not Browning Enough: If your soda bread isn't browning evenly, make sure your oven temperature is accurate. You can also brush the top with a bit of milk or butter for a golden finish.

Loaf Sounds Hollow: To check if the bread is done, tap the bottom; it should sound hollow. If it doesn't, return it to the oven for a few more minutes.

Chapter 18: Advanced Soda Bread Techniques

Shaping and Scoring

Once you've mastered the basics of soda bread, it's time to elevate your skills with advanced techniques in shaping and scoring. These techniques not only enhance the bread's appearance but also contribute to its texture and flavor. In this section, we'll explore how to shape and score soda bread like a pro.

Shaping Techniques:

1. Round Loaf:

The classic round loaf is the most common shape for soda bread. After mixing and lightly kneading the dough, shape it into a round ball. Flatten it slightly and use a sharp knife to score a deep 'X' on top.

2. Oval Loaf:

To create an oval-shaped soda bread, shape the dough into an elongated oval instead of a round ball. Score an 'X' on top or multiple diagonal slashes for an attractive pattern.

3. Mini Loaves:

Divide the dough into smaller portions to make mini loaves. Shape each portion into a round or oval shape, score as desired, and bake them for a shorter time than a full-size loaf.

Scoring Techniques:

1. Deep 'X' Mark:

The classic 'X' mark is not only traditional but also functional. It helps the bread expand evenly while baking, allowing the center to cook thoroughly.

2. Diamond Pattern:

Create a diamond pattern by scoring diagonal lines in both directions, intersecting at the center of the loaf. This design offers an attractive visual appeal.

3. Wheat Sheaf Design:

For a decorative touch, score the dough to resemble a wheat sheaf. This is achieved by making several shallow diagonal slashes around the loaf's circumference.

4. Heart Shape:

Show your love with a heart-shaped soda bread. Score two half-circles on top to create a heart, perfect for special occasions.

5. Floral Patterns:

Get creative with floral designs by scoring petals and leaves on top of the dough. This adds an artistic flair to your soda bread.

Decorative Loaves:

1. Braided Soda Bread:

For an elegant twist, divide the dough into three equal portions, roll each into a rope, and braid them together. This creates a visually stunning loaf with a unique texture.

2. Stuffed Soda Bread:

Take your soda bread to the next level by incorporating fillings like cheese, herbs, or nuts. Shape the dough into a round or oval loaf, add the fillings, seal the edges, and score the top.

3. Knot Rolls:

Create individual knot-shaped rolls by shaping small portions of dough into ropes and tying them in knots. Score them lightly before baking for added flair.

4. Twisted Loaf:

Make a twisted loaf by rolling out the dough into a rectangle, spreading your choice of filling (sweet or savory), and rolling it up. Twist the rolled dough into a rope-like shape and place it in a round or oval pan.

Chapter 19: Pairing Soda Bread with Dishes

Soups and Stews

Soda bread is a versatile companion that pairs beautifully with a wide range of dishes. Its crusty exterior and soft, crumbly interior make it a perfect match for hearty soups and stews. In this section, we'll explore how to pair soda bread with various soups and stews, enhancing your dining experience.

1. Classic Irish Stew:

Soda Bread Pairing: Traditional white soda bread is an ideal match for classic Irish stew. The bread's simple, slightly tangy flavor complements the rich and savory flavors of the stew. Tear off a piece of soda bread, dunk it into the stew, and savor the comforting combination.

2. Tomato Soup:

Soda Bread Pairing: Tomato soup's smooth and acidic profile pairs wonderfully with the mild sweetness of soda bread. Whether you're enjoying a creamy tomato bisque or a chunky tomato soup, a side of soda bread adds a delightful texture contrast.

3. Beef Stew:

Soda Bread Pairing: The hearty and robust flavors of beef stew find balance in the simplicity of soda bread. Its crusty exterior can be used to soak up the savory juices, while the tender interior provides a comforting contrast to the meat and vegetables.

4. Potato Leek Soup:

Soda Bread Pairing: Potato leek soup is creamy and velvety, and soda bread's rustic texture adds an enjoyable contrast. Spread a bit of butter on a slice of soda bread and dip it into the soup for a delightful combination of flavors and textures.

5. Lentil Soup:

Soda Bread Pairing: Lentil soup's earthy and protein-rich qualities are complemented by the mild and slightly tangy flavor of soda bread. Use the bread to scoop up the hearty lentil soup, creating a satisfying bite.

6. Seafood Chowder:

Soda Bread Pairing: Creamy seafood chowder with a medley of flavors from the ocean pairs wonderfully with soda bread. The bread's crusty exterior holds up well when used to scoop up the creamy soup, offering a delightful contrast.

7. Minestrone:

Soda Bread Pairing: Minestrone, a vegetable-packed Italian soup, is enhanced by soda bread's simplicity. Enjoy the harmony of the soup's hearty vegetables with the rustic charm of soda bread.

8. Chicken Noodle Soup:

Soda Bread Pairing: Classic chicken noodle soup is a comfort food staple. Soda bread's crumbly texture complements the tender chicken and soft noodles, creating a satisfying and wholesome pairing.

9. Chili:

Soda Bread Pairing: The bold and spicy flavors of chili are nicely balanced by the milder notes of soda bread. Tear off a piece of soda bread, dip it into the chili, and enjoy the fusion of flavors and textures.

Chapter 20: Beyond the Loaf - Soda Bread Desserts

Soda Bread Ice Cream

Soda bread may be known for its savory applications, but it also lends itself to delightful dessert creations. One such sweet treat is soda bread ice cream, a unique dessert that combines the comforting flavors of soda bread with the creamy goodness of ice cream. In this section, we'll explore how to make soda bread ice cream that will surprise and delight your taste buds.

Ingredients:

- 2 cups crumbled soda bread (any variety)
- 2 cups heavy cream
- 1 cup whole milk
- 3/4 cup granulated sugar
- 1 teaspoon vanilla extract
- 4 large egg yolks

Instructions:

1. Prepare the Soda Bread Crumbs:

Start by making soda bread crumbs. Crumble your leftover soda bread into small pieces. You can use any variety of soda bread, including white, whole wheat, or flavored versions.

2. Infuse the Milk and Cream:

In a saucepan, combine the heavy cream and whole milk. Heat over medium heat until it begins to simmer. Remove from heat and add the crumbled soda bread. Let it steep for about 30 minutes to infuse the flavors.

3. Strain the Mixture:

After steeping, strain the milk and cream mixture through a fine-mesh sieve to remove the soda bread crumbs. Press down on the crumbs to extract as much flavor as possible.

4. Prepare the Ice Cream Base:

In a separate bowl, whisk together the egg yolks and granulated sugar until the mixture is pale and slightly thickened.

5. Temper the Eggs:

Gradually pour the warm soda bread-infused milk and cream mixture into the egg yolk mixture, whisking constantly. This process tempers the eggs and prevents them from curdling.

6. Cook the Custard:

Return the combined mixture to the saucepan and cook over low to medium heat, stirring constantly, until it thickens slightly. Do not let it boil. It should coat the back of a spoon.

7. Chill the Custard:

Remove the custard from the heat and stir in the vanilla extract. Allow the custard to cool to room temperature, then cover and refrigerate it for at least 4 hours or overnight to chill thoroughly.

8. Churn the Ice Cream:

Once the custard is thoroughly chilled, churn it in your ice cream maker according to the manufacturer's instructions.

9. Add Soda Bread Crumbs:

During the last few minutes of churning, add the crumbled soda bread pieces to the ice cream, allowing them to mix evenly.

10. Freeze and Enjoy:

Transfer the churned soda bread ice cream to a lidded container and freeze for a few hours or until firm. Scoop and serve your homemade soda bread ice cream for a delightful dessert experience.

Soda bread ice cream is a creative and unexpected way to enjoy the flavors of soda bread in a sweet and satisfying dessert. It's a must-try for soda bread enthusiasts looking to expand their culinary horizons.

Congratulations on completing your "Soda Bread Cookbook" journey! Throughout this culinary adventure, we've explored the world of soda bread, from the classic recipes to creative variations and even unexpected desserts. Whether you're a beginner or an experienced baker, soda bread offers a versatile canvas for your culinary creativity.

In your soda bread cookbook, you've learned:

- How to bake classic soda bread varieties, including white, whole wheat, rye, and gluten-free options.
- Innovative ways to use soda bread crumbs for coatings, toppings, and more.
- Creative recipes for using leftover soda bread, from croutons to

bread pudding.

- How to make soda bread suitable for various dietary preferences, including gluten-free and vegan options.
- Advanced techniques in shaping and scoring to elevate your soda bread's appearance.
- Delicious pairings of soda bread with soups, stews, and other dishes.
- Unique dessert ideas like soda bread ice cream, showcasing the versatility of this bread.

Your soda bread cookbook offers a diverse range of recipes and techniques, ensuring that soda bread remains a delightful and essential part of your culinary repertoire.

Whether you're enjoying a warm slice of freshly baked soda bread with a pat of butter, dipping it into a savory soup, or savoring a scoop of soda bread ice cream, this humble bread has the power to bring comfort and joy to your table.

I hope you've enjoyed this culinary journey, and I'm here to assist you with any more culinary adventures or questions you may have in the future. Happy baking and cooking!

www.ingramcontent.com/pod-product-compliance
Lightning Source LLC
Chambersburg PA
CBHW051302160726
47994CB00003B/1273